Mountain Biking
around
North Yorkshire
Book 2

by

J.Brian Beadle

GW00417637

© J.Brian Beadle July 1995

Published & printed by Trailblazer Publishing
Stoneways, South End, Burniston, Scarborough. YO13 0HP

INTRODUCTION

This second book of mountain bike rides around North Yorkshire traverses the bleak moors and riggs around Glaisdale, Guisborough and the Hambleton Hills which contrast with the lush valleys of Ryedale.

It is adviseable to wear protective clothing eg. a cycling helmet, gloves, and good quality cycling shoes. Don't forget to take some extra warm clothing with you as well as food and plenty of drink. The moors can be unforgiving even in summer!

The maps in the book are drawn for guidance only and I strongly recommend that you consult the relevant Ordnance Survey map before setting out and take it with you. Some of the rights of way, although open at the time of writing, can be altered without notice, especially the ones in the forests. An up to date map can get you back home even if the alteration isn't shown. If you find you have strayed onto a public footpath please dismount. They are very much out of bounds to cyclists!

I hope you enjoy your riding as much as I enjoyed devising the routes and riding them myself.

And if you see me struggling up a long hill or gently rotating over the handlebars of my 'Kona' please take time to stop and pass the time of day, I'd love to meet you!

Cheers!

J. Brian Beadle
July 1995

ISBN 1 899004 09 2

CONTENTS

ROUTE 1

OVER GLAISDALE RIGG

Glaisdale is at the heart of the North York Moors National Park. Its lush green valley contrasts to the heather clad moor. Many years ago when the horse ruled as everyday transport, roads and paved ways were built over the moors. This ride uses some of these ancient tracks over Glaisdale Rigg and across to Great Fryup Dale.

- - - o O o - - -

FACT FILE
Distance - 15 miles (24Km)
Grading - Moderate
Off Road - 40%
Start/Grid Ref. - Glaisdale
OS Landranger 94 or OS outdoor Leisure 27
Grid Ref. 774054
Refreshments - Good pub (The Mitre Inn) in Glaisdale village
Excellent pie shop (Butchers near the pub)
You must try some of the marvellous pork pies!!
Pubs at Ainthorpe & Danby. Tea shop at the Moors Centre

- - - o O o - - -

The Route

Start in Glaisdale village and head off west towards Lealholm. At the edge of the village opposite High Leas farm go left onto a wide track signed as a bridleway. Go through the gate and keep straight ahead climbing uphill onto the moor. At the wide track go right then in 50yds. turn left onto the moor.

As the track falls it meets a wider track, turn right onto the track and climb back up onto the moor again. At the top turn left then where the track splits go right climbing up to the standing stone on the horizon at the road. Go straight across the road signed to Fryup, take care down the very steep hill with its severe corner. Look carefully for an unmarked road on your right and turn into it then shortly go left signed to Danby. At the next junction go left again signed to Danby then at the next junction bear right for Danby again.

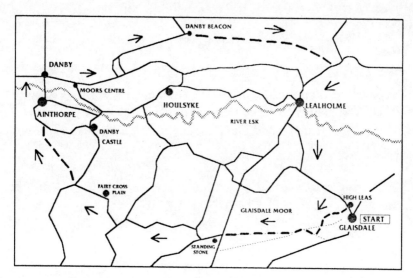

Carry on past Fairy Cross Plain to a junction of three roads. In front of you is a sign 'Bridleway to Ainthorpe', take this track which climbs onto Danby Rigg and eventually meets the road.

Bear left to Ainthorpe passing the Fox & Hounds on the way. At the junction continue along to Danby, cross the railway then turn right towards Lealholm. In less than a mile the road bends right at the Moors Centre. If you aren't visiting the centre go left here towards Lealholm up a steep hill. At the top turn left to follow the road all the way to Danby Beacon.

Go right at the beacon along a wide track for almost 3 miles to meet the road and turn right to Lealholm. Follow the signs from here back to Glaisdale.

- - - o 0 o - - -

The things they used to say!!

'Knickers', said George 'are the correct attire for cycling'.

c.1894

Cycling is a passion, not a pleasure!

c.1995

The Boneshaker is for imbecils!

c.1869

RAREFIED ROSEBERRY!

Roseberry Topping is a well known landmark around North Yorkshire & Cleveland. Its unusual shape was formed by mining many years ago. It rises 1057ft above sea level and there is a bridleway that reaches almost to the top. I won't ask you to ride it! But it would make an interesting descent!

- - - o O o - - -

FACT FILE

Distance - 17 miles (26km)
Grading - Easy
Off Road - 60%
Start /Grid Ref - Guisborough
OS Landranger 94 or OS Outdoor Leisure 26
GR 615158
Refreshments - The Cleveland Inn at Commondale

- - - o O o - - -

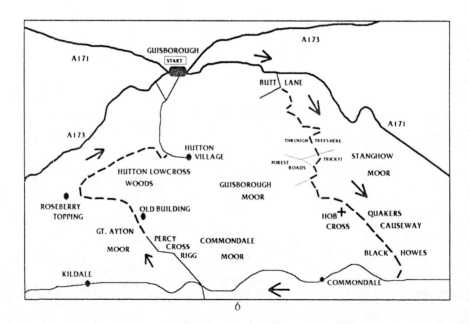

The Route

NOTE: This ride is undefined at times, please take the relevant ordnance survey map with you in case of difficulty

Start from the car park 100yds from the traffic lights when entering from Whitby. Ride back to the lights and in 100yds past the lights turn right along Butt Lane. When the road turns right go straight ahead along a wide bridleway. When the track forks go left and eventually enter the forest. Follow the blue arrow up the forest road and where it meets another road go left. In about 300yds turn right up a wide grassy path. Keep straight ahead at the next two junctions then shortly do a 'U' turn right up the hill following the blue arrow. Keep an eye out for a small clearing on the right, opposite this is a path up through the woods on the left. (If you miss the turning you will meet the Cleveland Way forest road which is out of bounds to bikers!)

Take this narrow path, soon crossing the forest road at the top onto another path. Follow blue arrows straight ahead to eventually meet a small gate. Through the gate the bridleway (not marked and quite undefined) goes diagonally right through the trees to exit onto a forest road. Left at the road then right as marked at the bottom of the hill. Over the bridge then left leaving the forest road for a track. In 100yds go right through the trees (bikers beware of a fallen tree) on a narrow track. Follow the blue arrows to eventually climb onto the moor along a narrow track. Follow the track passing Hob Cross on the right then keep along the line of the wall. When the wall goes left you must keep straight ahead towards the electricity pylons. The narrow track climbs and soon meets a paved way. Continue along this 'Quakers Causeway' towards Black Howes on the horizon to meet the road. Right at the road then right again in a mile signed to Commondale. Continue through the village (beware of steep hill) then at a crossroads go right up an unmarked road. Where the road ends go through a gate onto a wide bridleway towards an old building on the horizon.

Enter Hutton Lowcross Woods through a gate then turn immediately left. In about ½ mile turn left through a small gate onto the moor. Leave this track through another gate and ride down to the base of Roseberry Topping. Turn right at the obvious track which takes you through two gates into the woods. Follow the forest road back to Hutton Village, turn left at the road then right to take you back to Guisborough.

ROUTE 3

THE BAYSDALE BOG HOPPER

*B*aysdale, once the site of a secluded Abbey, now only a few stones remain in the farmhouse which is built on the site. This ride doesn't actually visit Baysdale Abbey but crosses Hograh Moor and Baysdale Moor on its way to meet Rudland Rigg. It is a hard ride and your skills will be tested to the full, but you will be thrilled by the descent off the rigg to Monket House and totally exhausted climbing the road out of Church Houses. Good luck!

FACT FILE
Distance - 28 miles (45km)
Grading - Rough & Tough
Off Road - 45%
Start /Grid Ref - Moors Centre car park near Danby
OS Landranger 94/717084
OS Outdoor Leisure 26 for detail over
Great Hograh Moor and Baysdale Moor
Refreshments - Pub and cafe at Danby, tea shop at the Moors Centre
at the start/finish, the Fox & Hounds Inn at Ainthorpe, the
Lion Inn at Blakey and the Feversham Arms at Church Houses.

The Route

*S*tart at the Moors Centre near Danby as there is a good car park and all the facilities. Leave the car park turning right and cycle to Danby. At the crossroads go straight across following the sign for Castleton. Pass through Castleton and as you leave the village at the speed limit signs take the first turn right signed to Westerdale & Commondale. In about a mile just after the cattle grid go left signed to Kildale then in almost two miles left at the 'T' junction signed to Westerdale. Follow the road downhill, over a ford then uphill. Near to the top of the hill turn right onto an unmarked road then look out for a bridleway sign on your right in a few hundred yards.

The real ride starts here. You will find it quite rocky and rough in places as you climb onto Great Hograh Moor to a technical descent to Great Hograh Beck. Cross the beck and turn right onto a track then in 100yds turn sharp left back on yourself to climb uphill onto a wide track. Continue uphill passing a large stone on the right then downhill, at a fork keep right then descend to pass through a hole in a wall to continue to the tree line. Go left now following a narrow undefined track parallel to the trees. The bridleway should climb off to the left in a few hundred yards but is completely undefined so you will have to guess the route and head off left through the heather to join a wide track. This

8

is the same wide track which you met earlier. It is not the right of way but is well used!

Soon you come to some shooting butts, at the third one (number 9) go sharp right onto an undefined track which becomes defined and soon joins up with a wide track once again. Keep on this track which eventually falls to Armouth Wath, keep right and head for the buildings. Pass over the small stone bridges then climb up again. In about 400yds the track forks turn left, then continue to ascend to Rudland Rigg. Left here and enjoy a good 4½ mile blast downhill along the Rigg. Look out for a wide track crossing the Rigg and turn left to enjoy a serious downhill bash to the road at Monket House. Right, then soon left to Church Houses then left signed to Castleton via Blakey. A long and arduous climb to blakey now. Left at the top of the hill then in 2 miles turn right signed to Rosedale. In 1½ miles turn left across Danby High Moor then at the road junction in 3 miles take the bridleway on the left signed 'Bridle-way to Ainthorpe'. At the road turn right and at the next junction at Danby Castle turn left to Duck Bridge. Cross the bridge and at the next junction go left to return to the car park.

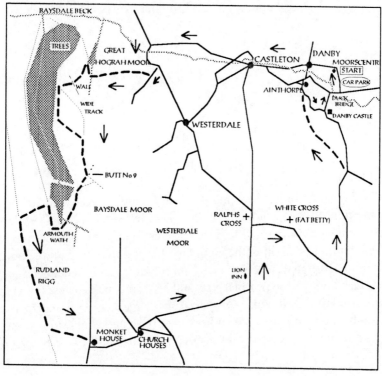

ROUTE 4

THE GOATHLAND GRIND

A tarn, three howes and an ancient cross are on this route. What more could you ask for! A blast over open moorland and a fast ride over the forest! You've got it! Then if you're feeling really fit why not combine it with ride 7 and have a real day out! If you do decide to, the only down (up) side is that you might get stuck in the Horseshoe Inn at Levisham supping superb Theakstons Old Peculiar!

- - - o o o - - -

FACT FILE

Distance - 15 miles (24km)
Grading - Moderate
Off Road - 45%
Start /Grid Ref - Goathland
OS Landranger/OS Outdoor Leisure 27
GR 830010
Refreshments - Pubs and cafes in Goathland

- - - o O o - - -

The Route

Start from the car park in Goathland and at the road turn right away from the Railway Station. Pass the Mallyan Spout Hotel turning right at the junction towards Egton Bridge. Shortly leave the road and turn left onto a signed bridleway heading up, and parallel to the road to a wooden sign for three bridleways. Go left here and climb to the ridge on an undefined path. Over the ridge there is a tarn on the right, keep left of the tarn on a wide track which climbs onto the moor to Two Howes Rigg. Keeping the howes on your left continue straight on heading towards Simon Howe on the horizon. At Simon Howe go right along a track for 50yds then immediately sharp left onto a track through the heather. You will see some posts across the moor in the distance which will guide you past a sheep bield on your way to Wardle Green. The moor ends at Wardle Green crossing a beck and exiting through a gate then climbing a rocky ascent between the edge of the forest and a field.

The route soon bears off to the right through a pair of old stone gateposts. Cross a field to a gate then diagonally right to another gate, eventually exiting through yet another gate onto a forest road. Cross the forest road and ride straight ahead between the trees and a fence to the forest drive road and turn right. Follow the forest drive for two miles until you meet another road. Turn right now onto the narrow road. In about four miles after the second set of double bends the road climbs, about a third of the way up the incline look for a wide track on your right, don't miss it. It is a sharp right turn onto the moor. The track goes round to a stile/gate then continues down to Hazel Head Farm on the right. Turn right through the farmyard, (please make sure to shut the gates), then continue straight ahead downhill through several gates to a stream Cross the stream,

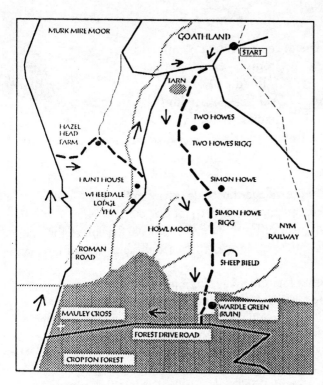

climb up passing through another gate then go right along an uphill track to the road. At the road go acute left then in one mile at the road junction turn right to return to Goathland.

HEARD IN THE WOODS!

Osh.......it!   A shout given by the common Black Backed Mountain Biker in the forest as he misjudges a downhill and sails gracefully over the bars onto the forest road. Sometimes nicknamed the Headbanger Bird because of the frequency with which he performs the trick!

11

THE SINNINGTON SLOG

This short run from Sinnington takes you onto woodland paths, narrow but rideable. It can be ridden with ride 8 if you want a longer slog. If you like old churches have a look into the crypt at Lastingham. It is reputed to be haunted. See if you feel the atmosphere as you descend into ancient history.

FACT FILE

Distance - 11 miles (17km)
Grading - Easy
Off Road - 60%
Start /Grid Ref - Sinnington
OS Landranger 100. GR 744858
Refreshments - Blacksmiths Arms Lastingham.
New Inn Cropton

The Route

If you are parking in the village choose your park with care. Head north on a narrow road keeping the pretty old school on your left. Shortly turn right towards the church at the 'No Turning Area' sign. Pass the church then where the road turns sharp right look to the left to see the old Hall, a fascinating building.

Soon you will see a sign for 'bridleway to Cropton' along a concrete road then across a field. At the far side of the field turn right following the blue way-mark. Shortly left along the bridleway then in a few hundred yards go right taking the obvious path into the wood. Where the path forks always take the right option eventually passing through a couple of small gates then a large one to cross a field to another gate.

Pass through the gate then immediately left through another gate at the blue waymark and down the hill.

This path is very wet in winter. There is a fallen tree across your path along here. Mind your head. YOU HAVE BEEN WARNED! Keep straight ahead following the occasional waymark to meet another track. Turn right here at the blue waymark and 'link' sign to a stile still keeping on the farm road until you meet the main road. If you wish to visit Cropton and the New Inn turn right up the hill.

If not, turn left down the hill towards Rosedale then at the bridge take the road on the left towards Lastingham. Carry on into Lastingham to have a pint

12

of Theakstons ale at the Blacksmiths Arms for some Dutch courage before exploring the crypt! Leave the village up the hill past the pub then at the junction keep left towards Spaunton. It's quite a hard pull up the hill, especially after visiting the pub! At the top of the hill where the roads bends sharp left go straight on along a white road, through a gate onto a wide track. In about a mile there is a junction of tracks. Go straight ahead here across a field. At the gate continue straight ahead onto a white road to soon meet the main

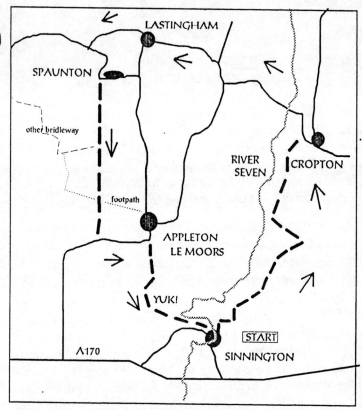

road. Turn left now towards Appleton le Moors. As you enter the village do not turn sharp left into the main street, instead go right along a bridleway onto a farm track as marked. Soon there is a choice of paths. Take the one on the right through the gate and across the field climb-ing to a small gate into the wood. It can be boggy here but persevere its not far! Through another gate then bear left and follow the waymarks to the river and Sinnington.

ROUTE 6

THE HAMBLETON HOBBLE

The Hambleton Hills were once host to an ancient highway called the Hambleton Road. Perhaps better known as the Hambleton Drove Road as it was used to drive cattle from Scotland to the more southerly markets. There were Inns along the route, alas long gone, and if todays travellers want hospitality they will have to make do with the Hambleton Inn near the start of the ride.

- - - o 0 o - - -

FACT FILE
Distance - 23 miles (37 km)
Grading - Moderate
Off Road - 50%
Start /Grid Ref - Sutton Bank car park near Helmsley
OS Landranger 100 or Outdoor Leisure 26. GR 514829
Refreshments - Pub at Hawnby.
Cafe at Sutton Bank Visitor Centre at the start/finish.
The Hambleton Inn just down the road towards Helmsley

The Route

Leave the car park at Sutton Bank and head off along a quiet road at the rear following the sign for Old Byland, Cold Kirby and Hawnby. In about half a mile go left signed for Hawnby and Boltby. In a few yards turn left onto the wide bridleway at Dialstone Farm. The road past the farm is the Hambleton road but you can take a more scenic route along Boltby Scar. At a kink in the path keep straight ahead following a sign for 'Jennetts Well'. At the edge of Whitestone Cliff turn right along a wide path. Below you is the supposedly bottomless Lake Gormire. The views from this point are amazing, on a clear day the hills of the Yorkshire Dales provide a backdrop to the flat valley below. As you ride the cliff edge take care and keep to the right if the path forks. After passing Boltby Scar, a steep wall of rock, the path passes through a small gate then going between a wall and a fence and eventually into a field. Keep to the wall on your right and head towards a barn on the horizon. Pass to the left of the crumbling old barn keeping near to a fast disappearing wall on the right.

Exit from the field through a gate then turn right along the road. At the crossroad go left along a wide track. This is the Hambleton Road.

14

Enjoy your ride along the ancient highway keeping straight ahead at all times. It is 6 miles to the end of the off road section over Black Hambleton where you join the road. Turn right here then continue all the way to Hawnby village. Go right and then left through the village exiting over the bridge towards Old Byland. Climb up through Cliff Wood then at the entrance to Murton Grange turn left. Shortly when the road goes right you must keep straight ahead into the field along a bridleway. Pass through a gate then take the right fork for a few yards then turn left at the Cold Kirby bridleway sign. At the wide track go left then left again where the track splits signed to Cold Kirby. In 100yds go left at the bridleway sign to cross a bridge and start a seriously steep climb up the other side of the valley. If you ride this you must be fit, or daft!

Most of us however will have a rest at the 'Captains Seat' two thirds of the way up! At the top of the hill cross the field to meet a road. Turn right onto the road and in about a mile left for a mile then right just past Dialstone Farm to return to the car park.

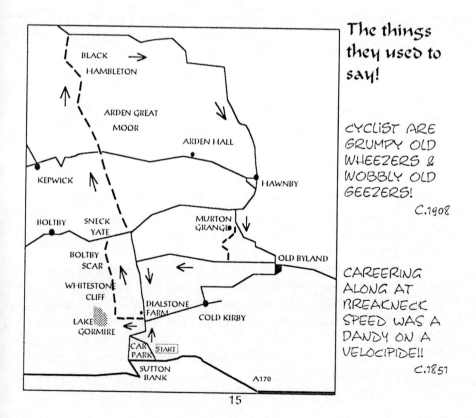

The things they used to say!

CYCLIST ARE GRUMPY OLD WHEEZERS & WOBBLY OLD GEEZERS!

C.1908

CAREERING ALONG AT BREAKNECK SPEED WAS A DANDY ON A VELOCIPIDE!!

C.1851

15

ROUTE 7

GOING LOCO AROUND LEVISHAM

Levisham, in the heart of the North York Moors makes a superb starting point for this ride. Please park with respect for the residents, it is advisable to arrive early at this popular venue. There are a couple of good downhill sections I am sure you will enjoy and you might even see a steam 'loco' on the way!

If you would like a longer ride combine this one with ride four to Goathland.

- - - o O o - - -

FACT FILE

Distance - 14miles (23km)
Grading - Moderate
Off Road - 50%
Start /Grid Ref - Levisham
OS Landranger 94/OS Outdoor Leisure 27
GR 833905
Refreshments - Horseshoe Inn Levisham,
White Swan Hotel Newton on Rawcliffe

- - - o O o - - -

The Route

Levisham village becomes quite busy and parking is at a premium, it is advisable to make an early start. Just before the Horseshoe Inn turn left along a small dead end road. Where the road finishes it becomes a track and a bridleway arrow points you to the right. Shortly the track forks, take the right one then in fifty yards go right again to enjoy a good downhill, but beware, there is a gate at the bottom!

Just a little further then do a 'u' turn to the left to join a narrow track over the field. Eventually enter a wood and follow a mixture of bridleway arrows and signs for the newtondale horse trail. Keep straight on to Farwath, bearing right through a gate and stream, cross the railway track with caution then right again over the bridge. Join a wide forest road now for an exhausting climb. At the top of the hill go right following a bridleway sign and a peculiar wood sign with a ruin on it! The track eventually becomes Tarmac and turns left at East Brow Farm/House to meet the road. Turn right here to Newton on Rawcliffe for refreshment.

When leaving the village at the outskirts look out for two wide tracks on your right. Turn right onto the tracks then take the left fork signed, Cropton 6 miles. This is a superb downhill, but beware of the steps and the gate at the bottom! Follow the track slightly right now up a short hill and traverse Stony Moor. Good luck! You'll need it as there are some right old ankle crackers over here! However the track soon comes out onto a farm road, go straight across through a gate following the link sign. In 300 yds. go left as instructed and follow this track to the forest road. Go left again and in a few yards turn right at the road towards Stape. In about a mile at a short downhill to the double bends carefully turn right signed to Raindale only. This road becomes a forest road marked as a bridleway shortly. Follow the blue arrows straight ahead to eventually arrive at a steep downhill at the picnic place of Raper's Farm. Make sure you go right here and enjoy a long downhill to Levisham Station, *BUT BEWARE OF ONCOMING TRAFFIC.*

Cross the railway line carefully then proceed uphill to return to Levisham and perhaps some refreshment at the Horseshoe Inn.

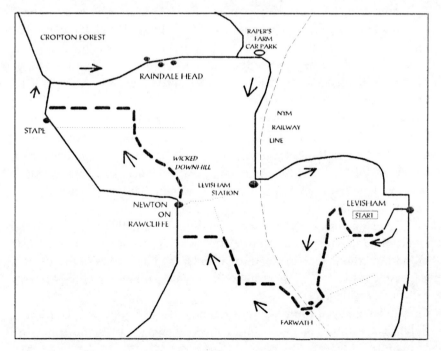

RIDE 8

OVER SPAUNTON MOOR

*A*nother short ride but with an exhilarating downhill section. It might be a good idea to have a full day out and visit the museum at Hutton le Hole, before the ride of course! If you would like a longer bash combine this one with ride six.

- - - o 0 o - - -

FACT FILE

Distance - 12 miles (19km)
Grading - Moderate
Off Road - 60%
Start /Grid Ref - Hutton le Hole
OS Landranger 100. GR 705900
Refreshments - Blacksmiths Arms Lastingham
Pub and cafe's in Hutton le Hole

The Route

Starting from the car park in Hutton le Hole turn right away from the village up the hill. In about a mile at the 'T' junction go left towards Lastingham passing straight through the village, without calling at the Blacksmiths Arms. In about one mile when the road goes sharp right (don't miss it), you must turn left onto a white road and eventually a bridleway. At the gate take the track uphill over the moor on the left.

It is a long slog for some way now as the bridleway reaches the heights of Spaunton Moor. Keep to the obvious bridleway and eventually you will see on the horizon in front of you the remains of a fallen cross. You need to turn left before this, look out for a wide track going left across the moor. This is a thrilling downhill bash, but take care it is a multi user track, especially at the Lastingham end where there are often children.

You leave the moor through a gate then ride down to the village. Turn right and continue past the Blacksmiths Arms, or nip in for a quick one, then up the hill to a junction. Take the road to Spaunton and at the top of the steep hill where the road goes left go straight ahead onto a white road then through a gate onto a wide track.

In about a mile you come to a junction of tracks (as in ride six). This time go right, it is a simple matter of following bridleway arrows and signs firstly across a field keeping to the right to exit into a wood through a small gate. Turning right into the wood just follow the blue arrows as the wide track twists and turns back to Hutton le Hole. At the road turn right to return to the car park.

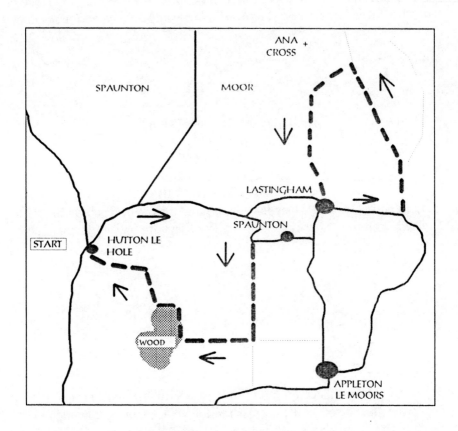

Topical Tips!

When riding in cold weather a cyclists feet are often the coldest part of his anatomy. Wearing a plastic bag on your feet inside your cycling shoes will help to keep out the cold and are a simple throwaway solution!

ROUTE 9

THE HARWOOD HUSTLE

You will not only hustle along the road to Harwood Dale but you will have hassle on some of the tracks which have been used by our four legged friends. Lumps and bumps are the order of the day, not to mention a good portion of mud. Perhaps if these tracks are ridden fast you won't feel the bumps! Except the ones on your head when you hit the ground! Good luck!

- - - o 0 o - - -

FACT FILE

Distance - 15 miles (24km)
Grading - Moderate
Off Road - 50%
Start /Grid Ref - Burniston
OS Landranger 101/GR 015928
Refreshments - The Three Jolly Sailors and Oak Wheel pubs at the start.
The Falcon Inn, Shepherds Arms & The Hayburn Wyke Hotel on route.

The Route

Start from the village of Burniston, perhaps leaving your transport on the wide grass verge on the approach to the village from Scarborough on the A165. Ride through the village turning right at the junction with the A171 past the Three Jolly Sailors. A few yards past the garage on the left turn left onto the Harwood Dale road. Bear right at the next junction eventually bearing right again climbing a steep twisty hill at Lindhead. Continue straight ahead for two miles then just past Grange Farm a few yards before a severe left bend turn right along a signed bridleway into a field. Pass through a gate into the forest keeping straight ahead and using your skills through the boggy woodland. Left at the forest road then right in a few yards along a wide un- marked bridleway through the trees at the top of the hill. Follow this rough track to meet a forest road at the farm turning right then left in a few yards at the blue arrow along a rough downhill to the road. Cross the busy road with care turning right onto a small road then right again before the Falcon Inn. At the top of the hill turn right then in less then a mile just past Tofta Farm look out for a wide signed bridleway on the left. This is ROUGH, it really shakes your bones about! Pass through a couple of gates into a field keeping straight ahead then through the farmyard to the road.

Turn right along the road passing the Shepherds arms. I said PAST the Shepherds Arms! Continue down the hill but before you reach the bend turn left at the sign for the Shire Horse Farm. At the telephone kiosk go left down the side of the bridge onto the railway line and turn right. A good blast now along to Hayburn Wyke but please be respectful to others, this is a multi user track. At Hayburn Wyke pass through a gate at the old station house. Then just before the next gate turn left, you can now have that pint at the pub!

Return to the track turning left through the gate and continue to Cloughton. Cross the road diagonally right then left past the old station, now a private house, to return to the track again which finishes at Burniston at the A165.

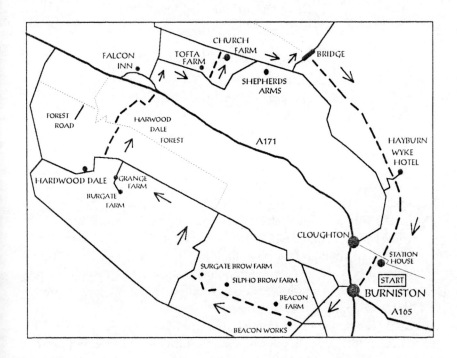

ROVTE 10
THE SLINGSBY SLAMMER

Some of the prettiest stone buildings in Ryedale are to be seen on this ride. Starting from Slingsby take a look at its ruined castle which was built as a country house around 1642. At Nunnington there is a fabulous Hall. A fine example of a manor house of the 17th century. But the jewel is Hovingham's superb Hall built in 1760 and dominating the village. However, by the time you reach Hovingham you will have mud in your eyes and probably too tired to bother with architecture! Although there is a possibility you might have fallen off at the Ford through Marrs Beck and be glad of a sit down to admire the view from the cool waters!

- - - o 0 o - - -

FACT FILE

Distance -14 miles (23 km)
Grading - Easy
Off Road - 50%
Start /Grid Ref - Slingsby
OS Landranger 100. GR 699746
Refreshments - Cafe & pub in Slingsby
The Malt Shovel at Hovingham & tea rooms
Pub at Nunnington

- - - o 0 o - - -

The Route

After finding a suitable street park in Slingsby head off through the village away from the B1257 towards Nunnigton and the twins, East & West Ness. Pass through East Ness then just before the road bends acutely right for West Ness at the Nunnington junction turn left onto a wide public bridleway and follow the blue arrows climbing all the way to the top of Caukleys Bank giving superb views across the valley.

Cross carefully over the road here to rejoin the bridleway to descend now into Stonegrave and its interesting Saxon church. Turn left at the road, (take care very busy in summer) then soon turn right as signed to Cawton and Gilling. At Cawton, on a sharp right bend, go left along the drive to Spa House. It is signed as a bridleway and Ebor Way. Keep on this bridleway all the way to Hovingham exiting through a gate. Take the obvious road into the village turning right through the water splash. Go right at the road, once again I ask

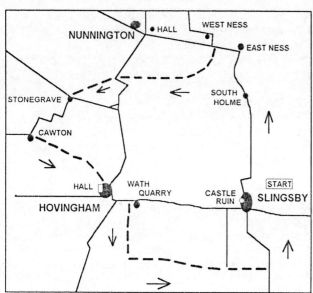

you to take care, then in less than a mile turn right at the bridleway sign alongside a house just before Wath Quarries. It is a wide track that leads to a field. Keep straight ahead and exit through a gate turning left onto a wide bridleway. Keep straight ahead at the gates to eventually reach the Slingsby to Castle Howard road. Turn left at the road to return to Slingsby.

The things they used to say!

Cycling any distance results in wear, tear & exhaustion. c.1895

Cycling can cause pelvic disorders, especially in young women. c.1892

"I have been told of a strange machine that goes without horses." c.1768

RIGHTS OF WAY

- ♦ BRIDLEWAYS - (Blue markings) Open to cyclist, walkers and horses.
- ♦ BYWAYS - (Red markings) Open to cyclists, walkers, horses and some traffic.
- ♦ PUBLIC FOOTPATHS - (Yellow markings) No cycling.
- ♦ OPEN LAND - Moorland, farmland etc. No right of access unless permission from landowner is obtained.
- ♦ TOWPATHS - Some are available for cycling without restriction, some are not. Others need a cycling permit available from British Waterways.
- ♦ PAVEMENTS - No cycling.
- ♦ CYCLE PATHS - Watch out for these marked paths. Information usually available from Borough and County Councils. A book containing cycle-paths in the North of England is soon to be available by the same author as this book.

CYCLING WITH SAFETY

- ♦ Prepare your cycle before riding.
- ♦ Carry spare clothing.
- ♦ Take food and water with you, even on the shortest ride.
- ♦ Always carry a good map and a compass.
- ♦ Take a whistle in case of emergency breakdown or injury.
- ♦ Always tell someone where you are going and what your expected time of return will be.
- ♦ Carry identification.
- ♦ Wear a helmet.
- ♦ Take care downhill especially off road, dismount if doubtful.
- ♦ Watch out for loose surfaces on corners.
- ♦ Learn first aid.

Books by the same author

Mountain Biking on the Yorkshire Wolds
Mountain Biking around Ryedale, Wydale & North York Moors
Walking to Abbeys, Castles & Churches
Walking on the Yorkshire Coast
Walking into History